Endorse

MW01172891

We were honored by a number of ministry and business leaders who were kind enough to endorse this book! We sincerely thank each individual listed below. Brief snippets of their endorsement are included here. For the full text, see www.manhoodjourney.org/dont-bench-yourself-book.

"This is a must-read for the fathers and mothers in the church!"
Nate Ashbaugh
Lead Pastor, Little Flock Baptist
Church, Louisville, Kentucky

"I was so encouraged by the simple, practical and spiritual wisdom . . ."
Dr. Jim Bechtold
Chief Innovation Officer, CEO Forum—Co-Founder
Crossroads Church—Vice Chair, World Vision US

". . . a wonderful book that will speak to you with much needed words of truth."
Matt Bell
Author of *Trusted: Preparing Your Kids for a Lifetime of God-Honoring Money Management*

". . . encouraged me to understand why I am tempted to give up."

Lawson Brown
Business Executive, and Cohost of the
Father On Purpose Podcast

". . . such an encouraging resource to me as a husband, father, and pastor."

Trey Brunson
Central Ministries Pastor, Church of Eleven22

"This book is a must read. It will help you get back up and keep going."

Paul Byrd
Former MLB All-Star Pitcher

". . . guides us in treating the problem and getting it right going forward."

Miranda Carls
Founder of Vertical Team and Leader Development,
Executive Director of Gateway Faith and Work

"My friend Kent's book will help us avoid poorly motivated self-benching!"

Pat Combs
Author of *More Than The Score: How Parents and Coaches can Cultivate Virtue in Youth Athletes*

"... a concise, thoughtful, wise, and practical resource ..."
Brian Croft
Executive Director, Practical Shepherding

"... you'll find encouragement and inspiration. A message we all need to hear."
Gregg Dedrick
Former President KFC, Author of *Building In The Spirit*

"This is more than a pep talk—this is God's proven game plan for victory!"
Michael DelGiorno
iHeart Radio National Morning Host

"Kent lays out strategies to get back into the battle when you feel like you've lost."
David Dusek
Author, Speaker, and Executive Director,
Rough Cut Men Ministries

"... practical tools wrapped inside engaging stories—a great read especially for parents!"
David Eaton
Cofounder and CEO, Axis.org

"Every second matters. Kent's book will help you make the most of them."

Tina Griffin

Founder of Counter Culture Ministries and
Host of the Counter Culture Mom Show
at www.CounterCultureMom.com

". . . a pleasure to read. It is casual and real and challenging and encouraging."

Mark Hancock

CEO, Trail Life USA and author of *Trail-Ready: 101 Devotions for Dads with Boys*

"Kent's new book will help you build character."

Dr. Chris Harper

Chief Storyteller & CEO, BetterMan

". . . as you read Kent's stories about his own failings, you'll be heartened."

Tom Harper

Author of *Servant Leader Strong: Uniting Biblical Wisdom and High-Performance Leadership*
and Founder, BiblicalLeadership.com

"I recommend this book, especially for parents, pastors, or leaders."

Dr. Jonathan Hayashi, Ph. D.

Lead Pastor, Sola Church and author of *Ordinary Radicals*

"My buddy Kent Evans nails it."
Jeff Kemp
Men's leader and Author of *Receive:*
The Way of Jesus for Men

". . . engaging illustrations and refreshing transparency, he connects and motivates!"
Dr. Ken Idleman
Vice-President of Leadership Development
for The Solomon Foundation

". . . provides biblical and helpful steps we can take to get back in the game."
Kyle Idleman
Senior Pastor, Southeast Christian Church and
bestselling author of *When Your Way Isn't Working*

"A shot in the arm that refreshes your soul. I highly recommend it."
Dr. Robert Lewis
Founder, Men's Fraternity, BetterMan and
author of *Raising a Modern Day Knight*

"Kent's honest storytelling and profound insights make this a must-read."
Nick Liberto
Executive Director of Proven Ministries

"You'll enjoy Kent's humorous style and delightful stories."
Scott MacLellan
Chairman Emeritus, TouchPoint Support Services and author of nine books, including *The Ancient Ladder*

". . . great job of weaving masterful stories with meaningful applications."
Don Manning
Founder and author of *Crazy Cool Family*

"The stakes are too high to quit. I encourage parents to read this book!"
Mark Merrill
President of Family First and All Pro Dad and author of *All Pro Dad: Seven Essentials to Be a Hero to Your Kids*

". . . a practical path forward to get back in the game after setbacks."
Jay Millar
Coach and Author of *Be a Hero in Your Home—The Ultimate Playbook for Men to Succeed at Home, Work, and Life*

". . . a roadmap for those feeling sidelined by fear, shame, or failure."
Vince Miller
Author, Speaker, and Founder of Resolute

"Kent has taken a deep theological reality and exposed it in a practical way."
Scott Nickell
Pastor, Southland Christian Church

". . . lays out the path to walk that gets you back in the game."
Dr. Zeke Pipher
Pastor and Author of *In Pursuit* and *The Wild Man: A Clear Path for Guiding Boys into Masculinity*

". . . brilliantly demonstrates how we can choose to enter and remain in the game."
Joe Pellegrino
President, Legacy Minded Men

". . . a magnificent job encouraging us to stick with it, persevere, and hang tough."
Kurt Sauder
President and cofounder of Further Still Ministries, Co-Author of *Getting Equipped*

". . . essential for anyone taking that big step into their next adventure."
John Shibley
Founder of Last In Line Leadership

". . . an easy to read book with a powerful lesson."
Dr. Dann Spader
Founder, Sonlife and Concentric Global and author
of Like Jesus resources at likejesus.church

"In a world where it's so easy to want to give up, this book encourages us . . ."
Mitch Temple, LMFT
Executive Director, The Fatherhood CoMission

". . . a fun and inspiring guide for navigating our daily failures with grace and humility."
Ben Thornley
Vice President of Church Engagement,
Wycliffe Bible Translators

". . . honestly addresses some of our greatest personal adversaries . . ."
Darren Walter
Pastor, Current: A Christian Church

DON'T
Bench
Yourself

DON'T Bench Yourself

HOW TO STAY IN THE GAME
EVEN WHEN YOU WANT TO QUIT

KENT EVANS

DON'T BENCH YOURSELF

Trade Paperback ISBN: 978-1-7354817-6-0

eBook ISBN: 978-1-7354817-7-7

Published globally by Manhood Journey Press, an imprint of Manhood Journey, Inc., 212 Prestwick Place, Louisville, Kentucky 40243.

Manhood Journey and the Father & Son Circle Logo are both registered trademarks of Manhood Journey, Inc.

SPECIAL SALES

Copies of *Don't Bench Yourself* can be purchased at special quantity discounts when purchased in bulk by corporations, educational institutions, churches and other special-interest groups. Contact the publisher for information at info@manhoodjourney.org.

I dedicate this book to my lovely wife April—my biggest cheerleader who's always encouraged me to stay in the game.

Contents

"And let us not grow weary of doing good,
for in due season we will reap,
if we do not give up."

Galatians 6:9 ESV

Foreword

> *"Let me tell you something you already know. The world ain't all sunshine and rainbows. It's a very mean and nasty place; and I don't care how tough you are, it will beat you to your knees and keep you there permanently if you let it. You, me, or nobody is gonna hit as hard as life. But it ain't about how hard you hit. It's about how hard you can get hit and keep moving forward; how much you can take and keep moving forward. That's how winning is done!"*
>
> —ROCKY BALBOA

I have known Kent Evans since 1984, when our tight-laced L.L. Bean Bluchers stepped on campus as freshman at an all-boys high school in Louisville, Kentucky called St. Xavier. He was in my P.E. class, and I quickly noticed he was an undersized athlete with a tremendous heart and a personality that was stand-up-comedian funny. I can still pull up his unmistakable laugh from my memory files with little effort.

Those were great days as we awkwardly fought to discover who we were as young teenagers. We wondered what kind of friend, student, or man we might become. And, many of us pined for the days when we'd get those shiny braces off our teeth so we could maybe, hopefully, confidently ask a girl to dance with us at a school "mixer." Music reigned supreme in the eighties with the explosion of MTV. Mike Tyson made his debut. Reagan recovered from a gunshot and warned us about Russia. Rocky ruled the box office (again and again, with the sequels). U2 rocked Live Aid and Pete Rose chased Ty Cobb to become the new base hit king. Man, we were only half way through a crazy decade!

During our times in high school and college, there was no class on Fatherhood 101. We weren't given tangible examples of what a good father looked like or should be. I'm not sure why, maybe it was assumed we should just know from life experiences. Ironically, though, we all spoke English, we still took courses on American Literature, British Literature, Comparative Literature, Contemporary Literature, World Literature, Creative Writing, Journalism, Rhetoric, Composition, Poetry, Debate, AP English Language and Composition, AP English Literature and

Composition, and even a Foreign Language to graduate. Is understanding how to diagram sentences or write a short story more important than fatherhood?

We went our separate ways out of high school. After college, I discovered I'd missed on my prediction that Kent would become a stand-up comedian. Instead, he chose a successful vocation in the corporate world. I was fortunate enough to carve out a career in Major League Baseball to become an average pitcher with an All-Star wife named Kym. Kent used his charm and married up, too, with a brown-eyed, curly-haired girl named April. We both became Christians and started families. We reconnected years later through our shared passions for sports, friendship, marriage, fatherhood, and deep, meaty discussions on faith. Kent would eventually exit the corporate world one day telling me, "I am leaving my job to start a ministry that creates content to help fathers disciple their kids." So admirable, so cool, so adventurous and also—so needed.

I say "needed" because there is a bond that runs so deep between a father and a son or a father and daughter. It shapes us. Molds us. A father is nearly irreplaceable. And that's only from a personal level. Politically, world-renowned Harvard sociologist, Carle Zimmerman, said years ago after studying all major civilizations that every collapse of a nation or society always happens in the family first, not the military. And as Kent shares so clearly, "We have a fatherless epidemic in this country, not a motherless crisis." But why?

Being a former Major League Pitcher and now broadcaster, I'm often invited to charity events to play golf. Many times, I'm drafted in the early rounds because most pitchers are supposed to be great golfers. But I'm no Maddux, Smoltz or Glavine on the golf course. As a matter of fact, I'm AWFUL.

After the 3rd or 4th hole, when I've already lost five balls and have usually hit at least one satellite dish on the roof of a house, I start making jokes. When those jokes no longer go over well because it becomes apparent our team isn't going to be in the money, it usually turns into an awkward day and I drive home kind of sad. I didn't measure up.

So now, after years of this, when a sponsor calls to get me for a charity golf event, I just tell them, "No, I don't really play golf anymore. It hurts my back and arm too much." If I'm honest, I should really just say it hurts my ego. I'm not very good at golf, and let's be honest, every man wants to know he has what it takes in something. And if we're not good at whatever thing we are doing, we as men, usually at some point, just quit.

I think quitting is okay in some areas. You don't have to be good at chopping down trees or fly fishing or painting your house. But, fatherhood is near the top of the list when it comes to accomplishments in a man's lifetime. It needs to be treated as such. I know it's much harder than golf or mastering other skills I just mentioned. This only makes us more prone to turn away and look for areas where we receive praise and feel like we matter or are "good at something."

I think this is where Kent's book comes in. Even though it's not only for fathers, I hope dads pay close attention.

If Rocky Balboa is right—life is hard and it's going to knock you down and winning is simply getting back up—then, *Don't Bench Yourself* is a must read because it will help you do just that.

Get back up. Stay in the game. Keep going.

Paul Byrd
Alpharetta, Georgia
Christian, husband of Kym, father of sons Grayson & Colby, Emmy award-winning broadcaster and former MLB All-Star who can still hit 81 mph at carnivals

Introduction

"So, what do we do when we feel like we're moving backward?"

I was speaking at a men's conference in Michigan. In my final session, I opened the floor for a question-and-answer time. On a screen behind me, I had a slide with a diagram of maturity progression in our lives. Less mature on the left, more mature on the right.

A brave man in the audience raised his hand and posed the question. I could relate to his quandary. There were 160 men in the room with us, and I assumed they could as well.

We've all been there. Some days, we feel like we're moving forward. Others, not so much. I was looking into the faces as I said the first thing that came to my mind.

"Do any of you remember the New York Yankees shortstop, Derek Jeter?"

I was counting on a couple things.

First, given the average age of the men in the room, I guessed they'd remember this former major league Hall of Fame baseball player. He played during their era. And, second, they would probably like him. After all, I was in the Midwest. This wasn't Jersey or Boston. I'd have never mentioned a Yankee up there! Even I knew better than that.

Oh—and a quick aside. I realize you may be reading from outside America, and I further realize that baseball is sort of an "inside joke" we are playing on the rest of the world. Forgive me if you have to do some searching or ask a friend about the nuances of the Great American Pastime (aka, baseball).

I saw heads nodding after I mentioned this baseball legend, so I continued.

I said, "I loved watching him play baseball. He was an amazing mix of talent, hustle and passion. Plus, he had a knack for coming through in high pressure situations. Mr. Clutch, they called him. Yet, he didn't *always* smack in the game winning run. And, there were times when *even he* booted a ground ball or threw one in the dirt. When that happened, here's what he didn't do: *he didn't 'bench' himself*."

I hadn't planned on saying this. It just came to me. Seemed like a solid (and geographically safe) analogy.

The men appeared to resonate. More heads nodded. So, I pressed in further.

"When Jeter made an error, he didn't call a timeout, throw his glove down, and stomp off the field. He didn't quit. He didn't go sit down and tell himself how big a failure he was. How he'd never get this baseball thing right. He didn't *bench himself*."

I went a step further, "Yet, isn't this what many of us men do? We yelled at our kids last night, so we've decided to disengage as a dad. We weren't godly or kind to our wives, so we stopped trying as a husband. We were laid off—again—so we just quit delivering excellent work. What's the use? It's easier just to go land a new job and do the bare minimum. Why give the extra effort?"

I took one final swing. "But, you know what? Nobody told you to quit. Your wife didn't ask you to back out of being an engaged husband. Quite the opposite. She's begging you to stay at it. Your kids—even when they bristle—don't want you to hand in your dad jersey and walk off the field. They need you. Desperately. Nobody is asking us to stop playing the godly man game. We do that to ourselves."

Incidentally, here's some "inside baseball" for you on how I processed this interaction.

I had planned a lot of content for that conference. I'd crafted some snappy slides and even hired a pro to make them look stunning. I used amazing and alluring alliteration. I covered dozens of talking points over the four sessions I led. Memorable phrases, open-ended questions, personal stories and relevant illustrations. All my speaker gear crammed into one conference.

But, after the event, the men only wanted to talk about one thing.

They had benched themselves.

The game of life had become too difficult. Rather than keep playing, they figured it was easier just to walk off the field, metaphorically speaking.

Several guys approached me and said, "Man, I see it now. I've been benching myself. Thanks for that." They sounded like they'd rehearsed their lines and compared notes. Same story, over and over.

One guy shared about how he had disconnected as a father. He found it too hard, so he had stopped trying. One husband said that he'd withdrawn from his wife because he didn't know how to love her well. He let his lack of confidence cause him just to pull back. Men said they'd quit trying to be friends, work hard, read their Bible or be engaged leaders. One after the other, they talked about how they had benched themselves.

Men aren't renowned for their open and honest feedback. Getting them to share can be like pulling teeth. So, even though it was maybe only a dozen individuals, it felt like a chord had been struck.

Part of me wanted to fist pump and be glad! Yeah, baby! Go God! I love it when He takes something I've said and allows it to land well. I know that I am limited, finite and bound by my own communicative inadequacies. Any good message comes from Him, not me.

But, if I'm honest, part of me was like, *"Really? The one thing I just threw in there at the end? What about all the slides?! One even featured a Bob Ross painting! What about my key takeaways and punchy, thought-provoking questions? What about those eight words that all started with the letter C?! You know how long I was on Thesaurus. com finding those?!"*

Yet, like a badly thrown pitch, it hit me.

Those weren't *my* words. That wasn't *my* diligently crafted talk. I didn't plan, strategize, think, craft and shape *that* message.

That was something God wanted to share. He made it happen.

He inspired the guy with the question and gave him the boldness to ask it. He steered me toward an answer. He even made use of the thousands of hours of major league baseball I'd watched in my teens and twenties. He is the potter, and Chicago Cubs baseball on cable TV was the clay. He can do anything!

And, while I happened to be speaking to a room full of men, I know this isn't just a problem for guys. It's a problem for all of us, men and women alike.

But what does "benching" ourselves look like? What do I mean by that term? It can take many forms, but here are just a few examples.

You're the mom who compared herself to that other mom (again), and you've concluded you'll never measure up. You bench yourself by avoiding any more growth or learning. "Since I'll never be as (pretty, organized, calm, etc.) as her, I'll just quit trying."

You're the dad who became angry and said hurtful things (again). You bench yourself by just diving into hobbies or television when you come home. Instead of learning to rid your heart and mind of anger, you just withdraw and avoid contact.

You're the employee who gave great effort in the past, but you didn't get the praise you expected. So, you bench yourself when you decide to give minimal effort. You've traded doing your best with doing the least you need to do to get by.

You're the man who traded devotion for distraction (again). You gave in to that temptation, so now you bench yourself by figuring, "Why do I deny myself? I'm not hurting anyone." You indulge whenever you feel like it.

You're the woman who swapped discretion for gossiping (again). You bench yourself by not repenting and turning that off. "You know, last week, I crossed a line and I don't want to talk about that person again like that." You press on with the secret and destructive conversations.

You can see these patterns in your life, and in the lives of those around you. No one is exempt from this temptation to bench themselves.

Still, while it's a common challenge, in my seat as a fatherhood ministry leader, I see this tendency more among men than women. I think guys tend to have a lower tolerance for endurance and a higher rate of withdrawal. I have two easily observed data points to back me up.

First, women give birth.

Let's be real. If men were asked to push through that kind of pain, humanity may have died off a few millennia ago. Women seem to be biologically and emotionally built for endurance, determination, and recuperation. When I'm sick, I'm in bed for 48 straight hours. When my wife is sick, she's folding laundry, paying bills, cooking a meal for us (while double-batching it for someone sicker than her), and helping one of our boys with his math lesson. She's a perseverance powerhouse.

Second, the fatherless epidemic.

Do we have a "motherless crisis" in our country? No, we do not. We have a fatherless epidemic.

I could trot out statistic after statistic. Here's just a sampler. For the last 50 years, kids have increasingly grown up with no father in the home. It's estimated that 23% of American children live in single-parent households—80% of those are led by single moms[*]. Sadly, this is more than three times the global average of 7%[†]. This percentage was almost four times lower in 1960 than it is today. I could share many more equally sad and alarming data points.

The bottom line?

Statistically speaking, dads are an ever-growing collection of quitters. There's something about our culture, climate, and spiritual condition that tempts men to wrongly choose abandonment over responsibility.

----

[*] https://www.census.gov/data/tables/time-series/demo/families/children.html

[†] https://www.pewresearch.org/short-reads/2019/12/12/u-s-children-more-likely-than-children-in-other-countries-to-live-with-just-one-parent/

And the statement above may sound harsh. However, it's all too real to ignore. Men seem to be more willing than women to throw in the towel. This isn't intended to beat men up, but it should wake us up. I know men—fathers in particular—wonder if they have what it takes. And, I know it's tempting for husbands and dads to want to give up.

Maybe this hits close to home for you. Perhaps you can relate to the question the men's conference attendee posed? Maybe, you're still in the marriage or in the home, but you have spiritually or emotionally benched yourself. You're there, but you're not *really there*.

You didn't do it perfectly—again—so you've given up. You walked off the field.

When we blow it, we are tempted to chase the error with a destructive narrative. There are hundreds of ways this could show up. Here are just a handful of things we can tell ourselves when we fail:

- Someone else should just take over.
- My family would be better off without me.
- My kids should be raised by a different mom.
- My workplace needs a more skilled leader.
- My church needs a more flawless volunteer.
- My parents need a more perfect child.

These narratives, and their evil cousins, can cloud our brain. We become exhausted and disillusioned. Yet, there's a chorus of people in the stands who want us back on the field!

However, they may not be cheering out loud. They're busy too.

Your wife doesn't want you to quit trying to pursue and serve her, but she can barely keep up.

Your husband isn't hoping you dive deeper into the social media abyss, though he may not say it out loud.

Your kids do not want you out of their life or just to let them do whatever they want, but they'll act like it.

Your boss didn't give you that rough performance review so you'd pack your stuff and leave.

Your church attendees aren't hoping you cave in or flame out.

The list goes on. While the people in our lives may not be audibly urging us on, in their spirits, they want us in the game.

And, beyond even these earthly stakeholders, we're told to look across time and through history for inspiration to persevere. There's another group showing us the way and cheering us on.

"Therefore, since we are surrounded by such a great cloud of witnesses, let us throw off everything that hinders and the sin that so easily entangles. And let us run with perseverance the race marked out for us, fixing our eyes on Jesus, the pioneer and perfecter of faith. For the joy set before him he endured the cross, scorning its shame, and sat down at the right hand of the throne of God. Consider him who endured such opposition from sinners, so that you will not grow weary and lose heart." (Hebrews 12:1-3)

The author of Hebrews tells us of this great cloud of witnesses, including Jesus Christ Himself, as inspiration for us to not give up. We have modern-day witnesses, as well. These include our wives, husbands, kids, friends, in-laws, colleagues—even that random guy who follows you on social media. They're all hoping we stay in the game.

If you've ever been tempted to walk off the field and give up, this book is for you. And, if you're on the bench right now, this book is *really* for you. I want to help you stay in the game if you're tempted to quit. Or, get back in it if you've already been sitting for a while.

To do this, we'll first tackle some top reasons we tend to bench ourselves. We will look at four temptations which call out, asking us to quit. Four enemies of the persevering person.

Then, we'll look at steps we can take to fight those enemies and stay in the game. We need not give in, buckle under or tire out. We can be victorious.

There's so much at stake my dear brother or sister! When you stay in the game, or get back into it, a great cloud of people in your life will thank God for this.

Let's play ball.

SECTION ONE

Why We Bench Ourselves

Chapter One

Fear

My teenage summers were dominated by baseball. I loved it. I was a solid player. Well, in the "recreation league" sense. I'd make the all-star teams, bat in the high .200's, and was quick on my feet. What I lacked in height or strength, I made up for with effort, speed, and coordination. I clearly didn't have a future baseball career ahead of me. Yet, I was a reliable player who could contribute to a winning team.

When I was about 16, we were scheduled to play a cross-town rival with a star pitcher named Steve Dixon. Steve had a mean fastball. To give his power some context, pitchers in our league might throw fastballs that would max out around 70 miles per hour. That was considered a solid speed.

Steve could throw the low to mid-80s. He might've even hit 85 a time or two. The net effect? The baseball looked like a golf ball coming at you! It defied the laws of physics. What was this voodoo curse he put on the ball? And, why does the catcher already have it? Where was I when he threw it? I'm out? When did he throw the other two pitches? I just got up here, and already I'm done?

It was rough and, honestly, a bit scary. Batting against him was like entering an alternate dimension. Things moved faster in "Steve's universe." I had a singular game plan when facing him: don't die. I just wanted to get back to the dugout with my body intact. That was a win.

I faced him in a few games that summer. I may have had a grand total of eight or nine at-bats. As the season progressed, I grew bolder. "This time, don't die while swinging!" Let's try that. Then, I was courageous enough to swing *with my eyes open*. Progress.

I never notched a hit against Steve. I didn't get on base even once. I struck out almost every time. But, eventually, by choking up and opening my stance, I was able to catch up to the pitches and foul some off. Contact! And I didn't die! Double win.

I'll never forget my final battle with him. I hit the ball! Wait, there's more. It actually went between the white lines! It flew deep to center field only to be snagged by the out-fielder on the warning track. I nearly blasted a home run off of him. I was never happier to be out (and unharmed). At least I went down in style.

FAILING OUR WAY TO SUCCESS

I learned two key things that summer. First, I can fail over and over again, but get better in the process. I could fail my way to success, so to speak. And, second, with enough at-bats, I could make something happen. Each one inched me closer to success. I'll bet you Steve would've *actually had to try* if I'd have had just one more game to dial in my swing.

Incidentally, by the end of that summer, guess what a seventy-mile-per-hour pitch felt like? A piece of cake. By failing (often) at a higher level of challenge, I was actually learning how to succeed in more everyday settings. I was growing my skill and capacity *while failing*.

For most of us, we're routinely presented with new challenges in life.

You might be a parent of teenagers. You now realize the stakes are higher, and their choices are wider. You want to keep the relationship intact, but it seems harder as they become more independent. The ways of parenting them when they were six don't work when they're 16. Friends, social media and these things that kids call "opinions" add a degree of difficulty to your role as a father or mother.

Maybe you've bumped into health challenges. You've never had these before. Your spouse has chronic pain. You need to make dietary or exercise changes. Your parents are aging, and hard choices are looming. You once could rely on your health; but now, it's becoming an unwelcome factor in many of the decisions you make. What you took for granted is no longer a guarantee.

Perhaps your career is going well. This is creating more opportunities. Only, they require an expanded set of skills you must learn. The old ways of working are failing you. You've never had to lead so many people. This is the biggest budget you've ever managed. In addition to being functionally skilled, you now must also have crucial conversations, coach your team, resolve conflict and manage "up" to higher-profile executives or Board members.

Metaphorically, you're trying to hit harder, tougher pitches. You are on the edge of a new future. You can see them coming faster and faster. And you have this growing sense that the costs of striking out will increase.

You could alienate your son or daughter, push them away for a decade or more. You want to be an engaged parent, but it's difficult.

You might not be ready for the bigger job, and this will only expose your insecurities or skill gaps. You feel professionally off-balance.

You and your spouse are walking through new seasons. You want to be there for them, you just don't know how.

You're headed into uncharted territory. And it scares you.

So, here is the temptation: just quit now. Before we get fully involved in this faster-paced game, we give up before we start. Our fear keeps us from stepping up to the plate at all. It's safer here in the dugout.

You decide not to have children because you just don't know if you can be a good parent. You decline the new role because you're not sure you can deliver. You hide in your hobbies because it's easier than serving your spouse when they're not at their best. You double down on the dictatorial approach with your teenagers, even though it's driving them further away.

We can sometimes sabotage our own growth because we're afraid we won't be able to play the game of life at the next level. We'd rather win at "JV" than risk the loss at varsity. Fear of failure, exposure, or the unknown can paralyze us. We bench ourselves, even before the first pitch is thrown.

NURTURING A DIFFERENT SPIRIT

There is an amazing story in the Bible about a group of spies sent to scope out some land. You'll find it in Numbers 13–14. The short version is that God had promised to give Israel an abundant and blessed plot of land. As they assembled on its borders, their leader, Moses, sent 12 men to check out the land and report what they found. They were gone for 40 days.

Upon their return, 10 of the spies saw it one way. Only two—Joshua and Caleb—saw it differently. The majority agreed the land was good, but they also believed it was too dangerous to conquer. In one of those unfortunate lists in the Bible, these fearful spies have their names captured for all of us to see for all time. Ouch.

They said things like: the people who dwelled there were "strong" and "of great height"; the cities were "fortified and very large"; the land "devours its inhabitants." (Numbers 13:25-33). They gave a bad report. They went so far as to stir up the people, suggesting they should just return to Egypt. They threatened to kill Caleb and Joshua for disagreeing with them!

God Himself intervened to stop the madness. He said he would disinherit Israel and basically start over. But, Moses pleaded, and God relented. Instead, God implemented a rather unique punishment. He would let a whole generation (everyone over the age of 20) die off before Israel would enter the land. He would only let the younger crowd in. But there were two spies God exempted from this consequence: Caleb and Joshua. They were the only plus-20s who would see the Promised Land (Numbers 14:24).

If my generation were ever tested, and a whole crowd of us were fearful doubters, I'd love to be listed as an exception. We can sometimes find comfort in the crowd or see safety in numbers. But Caleb and Joshua were different. They had a different viewpoint. We must be like Joshua and Caleb.

Caleb was specifically called out by God. The Lord said he had "a different spirit and has followed me fully" (Numbers 14:24). He had the spirit of faith, not fear! God singles Caleb out. A man of a different spirit.

Caleb didn't have a spirit of faith *in himself.* He had faith in God! Caleb wasn't going to rule the day, rise and grind, take the hill or pull himself up by his own bootstraps. It wasn't just that he had a spirit of faith. It was where he put his faith that mattered! In whom. In God! Not himself.

Our culture will tell us to have faith. In ourselves. In our government. In others. You do you. Trust fate or karma or good intentions. But, the truth is that we must have faith in God. Alone.

We must resist the temptation to play the game by our own strength. Sure, we can leverage the skills and talents God has given us. That's good stewardship. But do you know what's better than all our skills, strategy, and striving? God's favor! Knowing that He is with us. He will never leave us or forsake us. We can know that as we fail—and we will at times—we are building faith and experience muscles that will serve us well in the future.

The spies who doubted God were fearful. They saw the obstacles in the foreground and shoved God's power to the background. They focused on the size of their opponent, not the size of their God.

The only kind of fear we want to carry around with us is the fear of the Lord. It's the beginning of wisdom (Proverbs 9:10). Almost all our other fears—of people, situations, outcomes, or even our own future—are unhealthy and spawned by our enemy. We do not walk in fear. Let's be like Caleb and have a different spirit.

As Paul told Timothy, we should fan into flame the gifts God had given us "for God gave us a spirit not of fear but of power and love and self-control" (2 Timothy 1:7, ESV).

Don't let fear drive you to bench yourself before you even begin.

Chapter Two

Shame

If fear can't convince you to stay on the bench, shame will try to make you a one-play performer.

Fear wants you to see the opposing team and never put your jersey or cleats on. If that doesn't work, the enemy will ask shame to step in. Shame will let you give it a go—just so you fail. Then, shame will remind you of how exposed, weak, insecure, and pathetic you are.

Fear is a dream killer. Shame is an embarrassment tiller.

It digs up your insecurities, memories, and past blunders. Then, it bunches them together with your most recent failure. If fear can't keep you from starting, shame will keep you from continuing. Fear keeps you hidden, while shame exposes. Fear keeps us out of the spotlight. Shame splashes our errors on the jumbotron.

SHAME SEEKS TO SIDELINE US

You may have faced a fear, chased a dream, or attempted a mission. Before long, though, you blew it. You jumped into the game, but sure enough, you mishandled one of your early opportunities. "Put me in, coach!" quickly became, "Where can I hide?" You were willing and ready to brave the new path. But soon you were faced with the exposure of a mistake you couldn't hide.

You took over the business unit, only to see key staff hit the exits as the numbers tanked. You became the new pastor, then watched your church split over the transition. You're the mom who stepped into the relational mess your daughter was enduring, only to make it worse as her friends further alienated her. You tried to be an engaged dad by bringing up sexual integrity with your teenage son, only to be pushed away.

You wanted to love your wife well, but your well-meaning "feedback" came out as harsh criticism. You thought you were helping your husband become more engaged as a dad, yet you were just pointing out how far behind he is in the fatherhood game.

We've all been there. We've felt the deep shame of failure. Sometimes, we have great motives, but the execution is off. Right idea, wrong method. But, if we're honest, the ones that really sting are those where our intentions weren't lily white.

We were caught fudging that expense report and got fired. Now, we find ourselves looking for our next opportunity while not being super honest about our reasons for leaving. We became angry over something insignificant, and now we're more alienated than ever. We ventured into a dark place online, and our spouse was hurt and angry. We chased financial success, while our kids looked into the stands, seeing not just a vacant seat, but an empty promise.

TWO FLAWED, BUT ENCOURAGING, EXAMPLES

When I look to the Scriptures for encouragement in overcoming shame, I find the stories of two individuals most helpful: David and Peter.

I find it interesting that both of these men had colossal failures recorded in the Bible. Yet, we see David labeled a man after God's own heart (1 Samuel 13:14; Acts 13:22), and Peter mentioned as one of the key leaders through which Christ would build His church (Matthew 16:18). These men stepped into massive, humanity-altering leadership roles, only to come face to face with their own inadequacies. They persevered despite themselves. Let's take a closer look at how they did it.

DAVID MOVES PAST HIS SIN

David defeated Goliath. Odds are, this is a story you've heard. The young shepherd boy took on the Philistine champion. He defeated him; and, in the process, he acknowledged that it was God who brought him the victory. David went on to display honor and courage as he was unfairly hunted by King Saul. Even when he had the chance, he didn't take Saul's life, because he dared not lay his hand on the Lord's anointed. He was a fearless warrior, slaying his tens of thousands, along with lions and bears. He fought for God, wrote many of the Psalms, and led Israel to many victories.

Yet, like all of us, he was also flawed. One of his most egregious series of errors is captured in 2 Samuel 11–12. I'll summarize the story for our purposes here.

As king, he saw an attractive woman bathing, took her, and slept with her. She became pregnant. Adding to the depth of sinfulness, she wasn't just a random citizen. She was the wife of one of his mighty men, his inner circle. Doubling down on his error, he had this man—one of his closest allies who had pledged his life to defend David— intentionally killed in battle.

In this one story we see a series of despicable mistakes. He abused his position as king, betrayed a friend, committed adultery, and had an innocent man murdered. It would be difficult to stack more sin into one series of events. Thou shalt not covet, kill, lie, or commit adultery just to name a few. David covered all the despicable bases in a short span of time. Only when confronted by a courageous advisor, did he see his sin and repent.

Interestingly, after this debacle, he wrote Psalm 51. It's worth a close read, especially if you're walking in shame right now. In it, David poured his heart out to God. He acknowledged his sin. Then, in a series of bold statements, he requested some amazing provision:

- "Have mercy on me, O God" (verse 1)
- "Blot out my transgressions." (verse 1)
- "Wash me . . . cleanse me from my sin!" (verse 2)
- "Create in me a clean heart" (verse 10)
- "Cast me not away from your presence" (verse 11)
- "Take not your Holy Spirit from me" (verse 11)
- "Restore to me the joy of your salvation" (verse 12)

He didn't sugarcoat his sin ("Well, since I was trying my best") or pretend he was a victim ("She shouldn't have been on the roof out there for everyone to see in the first place"). He knew what he had done was disgraceful. He couldn't rewind the clock or rerun the play. Yet, he knew where to turn. Where to put his trust, hope, and future. Not in his ability to fix it, but in God's ability to turn it into something instructional and redemptive, as only He can.

He went on to mourn his behavior. He begged God for the life of his newborn son. Then, he accepted God's judgment when the boy was not allowed to live. David, a man after God's heart, clearly experienced deep regret. He felt crushing shame. Only with God's power to forgive and restore could he move on and experience life after shame.

PETER CORRECTS HIS COURSE

While the circumstances are quite different, we see a similar sin-shame-restoration pattern in the life of Peter. Like David, Peter was a key figure in the history of God's redemption story. He was one of Jesus's most trusted disciples. He helped launch the church and was faithful to Christ even to the point of a martyr's death. He had some amazing moments captured of his faith, courage, and insight. He walked on water (Matthew 14) and performed miracles (Acts 3). At one point, Jesus even commended his insight (Matthew 16).

Yet, as we look at shame, let's turn to perhaps Peter's lowest moment recorded in the Gospels. The night he denied even knowing Jesus.

You can see one account in Matthew 26. Jesus predicted, during His final meal, that Peter would deny him. Peter objected! He was almost certainly shocked, perhaps even offended by the accusation, saying, "Even if I must die with you, I will not deny you!" (Matthew 26:35)

Yet, as we see, Peter did just as the Lord predicted. After Jesus was arrested, Peter was accused of being with Jesus three separate times. Each time, he lied and ran for cover. His denials became even more animated, with Peter swearing that he didn't know Jesus (Matthew 26:74). At the moment Jesus most needed a friend, Peter became a traitor.

Yet, Peter's story doesn't end there! He is not remembered as one who abandoned Christ. Rather, he is remembered as the rock on which Christ built the church! He wrote letters we still have as part of our Bibles today. He died a martyr's death. He fed God's sheep. He is remembered as one of the fathers of our faith, despite his less than perfect track record.

WHERE SHOULD WE TURN?

In the lives of these two men, we see a number of principles for overcoming shame.

First: a blunt acknowledgment of our sin. David gives us a clear picture of this. He didn't hide. He confessed to the Lord, knowing that he had sinned against God. We'll look at this more closely in Chapter 5.

Second: a return to the Lord. Peter betrayed Jesus just as much as Judas had. The difference between these two men is found in where they turned after their sin. Peter turned toward Jesus. Judas did not.

Third: regrouping and restarting. These men didn't let shame keep them from taking the next step. David ruled and governed to the best of his ability. Peter shared the gospel and used his own story of grace to propel him toward increased commitment.

There are dozens of other examples in Scripture that highlight this same point. Shame is a tool of our enemy, designed to hold us back and keep us off the field. Shame is neutralized by humility. It's rendered powerless by confession. It's wiped away by God's grace.

The prophet Isaiah said, "But the Lord God helps me; therefore I have not been disgraced; therefore I have set my face like a flint, and I know that I shall not be put to shame. He who vindicates me is near. Who will contend with me? Let us stand up together. Who is my adversary? Let him come near to me. Behold, the Lord God helps me; who will declare me guilty? Behold, all of them will wear out like a garment; the moth will eat them up." (Isaiah 50:7-9 ESV)

If you're walking in shame right now, take your queue from Isaiah and the lives of David and Peter. Turn toward God, not away from Him. Lean into His grace. It's more than sufficient.

Chapter Three

Criticism

You are moving past fear and jumping into the game. Shame isn't sidelining you, and you're strengthening your spiritual muscles. Now, criticism steps in to try and wear you down.

You're answering the call, even though it still occasionally scares you. You've made mistakes, yet you've discovered that God's mercies are new every morning. But criticism is a new enemy.

Its *modus operandi* is different. It doesn't try to scare you or shame you. Instead, it beats you down. Death by a thousand cuts. Criticism plays the long game. With each passing day or year, it seeks to bury you under the aggregate weight of tons of small nits, digs, and pokes.

ALL CRITICISM, ALL THE TIME

On one hand, you're the athlete who wants to see the game film. You're open to feedback so you can learn, grow, and improve. On the other hand, would it hurt to get a pat on the back occasionally? Must it always be about our flaws and failures? How about just one atta-boy when we get it right? Is that too much to ask?

You didn't perfectly handle that dinner conversation, staff meeting, trip to the grocery, or financial decision. Everything's under the microscope. You feel as if every action elicits negative feedback. From your wife, kids, friends, boss, staff, or colleagues.

You want to keep swinging, but all you hear are boos. Even when you get on base, they bark at you for not hitting a home run.

I recall a time when I worked for a terrific boss. He was a passionate Christian leader, capable, generous, and a ton of fun. He was so smart and driven, though, it seemed like he was incapable of delivering a simple compliment. He would regularly chase the kind word with, "and next time, let's see if we can . . .". Generally, I welcomed these added insights. But, one day, I decided to press him for a different approach.

He called me to his office to congratulate me on a small, but important, achievement. Then, he added one of his keen insights about how it could've been *even better*. We had a great relationship, so I jabbed a bit: "You just can't do it, can you?"

He looked back, confused. "Can't do what?"

"You just can't deliver a compliment without adding a critique, can you?"

He gave a sly smile. I doubled down and said, "Let's do this. I'll leave and come back in. You're gonna tell me, 'Nice job', and then, let me get back to work."

I stepped out of his office and hopped right back in, smiling. He blurted, "Beat it. Get back to work." We both laughed.

A decade later, I still count this man among my friends and mentors. That day, I sent the subtle message: Sometimes, it's okay to give a compliment without an accompanying critique.

Many of us work with people like that. Some of us *live* with people like that! No matter how hard we try, there's always criticism. To be fair, some of us need it.

FEEDBACK THAT HELPS

When April and I were first married, I was an irresponsible young man. I wasn't always honest either. I'd say traffic held me up (partially true) when I really had stuck around the office too long. I didn't pay bills on time. I'd stretched to buy a brand new car (out of my price range), and the five-year's worth of payments were burdensome. I had racked up credit card debt. I had a long way to go to become financially prudent, responsible, and honest.

My lovely wife would occasionally mention these things, and she was appropriately critical. I not only deserved the criticism, I needed it. I had to be shaken out of my immaturity!

My wife wasn't nagging me destructively. But, she did point out when I didn't live up to my own stated values. *She* wasn't the problem. The problem was my lack of integrity and follow through.

I have heard from thousands of fathers and husbands. I have sat in coffee shops with hundreds more. Some of these guys want to suggest their wife is always unfairly nagging them. They pull out Bible verses about a quarrelsome wife (Proverbs 25:24) or her being like a constant dripping on a rainy day (Proverbs 27:15-16).

Yet, often, these men are where I was (sometimes I'm still there!). They believe the issue is with their wives when the issue is often their own sin and selfishness.

If you're married, do any of these descriptions hit too close to home?

- You're overstretched financially. You made some bad choices, and now you're wrestling with crushing debt.
- You want to speak positively to your spouse, but you're frequently dredging up their past mistakes.
- You're not reliable. You don't come home when you say you will or tackle those projects as promised.
- You're living in blatant sin. You're addicted to pornography, gambling, or alcohol. It's become your pattern.
- You place work above your spouse. You can't recall the last time you shared a meal or date night when you didn't check texts or emails.

Please do not read that list as if you're being judged for it. As we will discuss in a couple chapters, calling it out is a key to getting past it. We don't want to confuse healthy conviction with unfair judgment. If some of those statements land hard, it may be a clue that you need to lean into that and ask yourself why.

In my case, I recall a number of times when my lovely bride's method of delivery wasn't precisely on point. Nevertheless, she was right. Just because she didn't offer the feedback on a fluffy pillow, didn't mean I should reject it. Her method may have been heavy handed, but her message was spot-on. I learned to receive the message and discard the method.

Maybe you're a husband engulfed in frivolous pursuits. You're irresponsible. Or, you're a wife who regularly overspends or burns hours each day scrolling the socials. You just want your spouse to mind their own business and stop throwing Bible verses at you about diligence, frugality, or self-control. But, they have a point, don't they?

We all need constructive criticism. You may prefer a more benevolent phrase, like "positive feedback." In any event, we need to be shaken from our sin patterns so we can turn to God's grace and walk worthy (Matthew 18, Galatians 6). Not all criticism is bad. Just because someone's critical doesn't necessarily mean they should be ignored.

FEEDING ON FEEDBACK

Proverbs 15 says, "The ear that listens to life-giving reproof will dwell among the wise. Whoever ignores instruction despises himself, but he who listens to reproof gains intelligence." (Proverbs 15:31-32). And in Proverbs 27, we see, "Faithful are the wounds of a friend; profuse are the kisses of an enemy." (Proverbs 27:6).

Sometimes, critical feedback is our best friend.

But, let's talk about the other side of the criticism coin.

None of us are flawless! Some of us have people in our lives who expect perfection. All the time. They never let up. They're convinced their role in life is to point out each and every moment we don't live up to their unrealistic standard. That's when the train careens off the tracks.

For some of us, we've tried and tried. We kept going out on the field and made some great plays! We notched base hits, snagged ground balls, and threw folks out. There was even that diving catch we made, stifling the other team's rally attempt. We stole bases and scored runs.

Yet after all that, we came into the dugout and saw the scowl on our coach's face. "You got that guy out, but sure cut it close. You poked that pitch up the middle, but if you'd have turned your hips faster, you'd have parked it over the left-center wall. If you'd have been quicker out of the box, you could've stretched that single into a double."

WHEN GOOD ENOUGH ISN'T GOOD ENOUGH

Nothing is ever good enough. There's no genuine praise. No atta-boys. No high fives. No recognition of how hard you work, hustle, or grind. You're not looking for a trophy every night when you walk in the door. But would it be okay to be met without a frown, harsh word, or critique?

I have worked for other bosses like that. They prided themselves on always asking about the one thing you didn't do. If you brought in eight ideas, they wanted nine. If you shared a 10-slide presentation, they asked for the 11th. If you made five calls above your quota, they wondered why it wasn't six. "How high did I tell you to jump? Then, why didn't you jump higher?" They can be exhausting.

Maybe you have a boss like that. Maybe you grew up with a dad like that. Or, just maybe, you're married to a spouse like that. Maybe you're like that?

Being around people like this can be discouraging and demoralizing. Eventually, it tempts even the most faithful person to give up.

Two Old Testament heroes come to mind when I consider the weight and pain of negative criticism. One is Job. The other is Nehemiah.

Job was challenged with unthinkable loss: money, family, cattle, friends, health. He had nearly everything taken from him. And we read that some of his so-called friends criticized him harshly. They even suggested that he was personally to blame for all this. On top of all that, Job's wife says, "Do you still hold fast your integrity? Curse God and die." (Job 2:9). Job suffered deep loss and heaped on top, plenty of criticism.

Nehemiah left his cushy palace job to rebuild the walls of Jerusalem. He went on to govern the city long after that. During the rebuilding, he was threatened and harshly criticized by a collection of bad actors. One of these men, Tobiah, called out, "What they are building—even a fox climbing up on it would break down their wall of stones!" (Nehemiah 4:3). Frankly, I think Tobiah's choice of insults is comical. I'm glad it's recorded for us. But, even though his curse game may have been lacking, he and his cronies turned up the heat repeatedly. He was a genuine threat.

I would argue that Job and Nehemiah show us two examples of how to handle harsh, negative, and ill-motivated criticism. In each case, these God-focused leaders remained steadfast, They trusted the LORD and stayed fixed on their mission. They tuned out the haters and kept their eyes on the prize.

Can you relate to the plight of these men? Do you have so much criticism swirling around you that you must fight to retain your balance and vision? Or have you already thrown in the towel?

Take heart. Even if criticism is raining down, you don't need to be swamped. You can let it roll off your back and not get lodged in your heart. With God's help, you can ignore the unwarranted negativity and rest in His love for you.

Paul stated this well in his letter to the Romans. Chapter 8 begins with, "There is now no condemnation for those who are in Chris Jesus." (Romans 8:1). He reminded us that condemnation has no place in the life of a believer. This chapter of Romans closes with Paul emphasizing, "What then shall we say to these things? If God is for us, who can be against us? . . . For I am sure that neither death nor life, nor angels nor rulers, nor things present nor things to come, nor powers, nor height nor depth, nor anything else in all creation, will be able to separate us from the love of God in Christ Jesus our Lord." (Romans 8:31, 38-39)

You may be on the receiving end of a load of criticism right now. But take heart, Jesus has overcome this world. Since this is true about us, we should never bench ourselves due to the criticism from others. We press on in light of the inseparable love of Christ.

Chapter Four

Impatience

Maybe you sailed through the first three chapters. Fear doesn't keep you from trying new things. Shame hasn't sidelined you despite your mistakes. You readily learn from good criticism, and ignore the rest.

You are fear-friendly, shame-shielded and criticism-conducive. You're rolling smooth, engaged in the game, and expecting big things.

However, it's *this very mindset* that threatens to sneak up on you.

You're moving quickly as a leader, husband, wife, or parent. One thing keeps you going. You've had plenty of it, and you're ready for more. One resource fills your tank; and, as long as you get enough of it, you'll plow ahead. But, if it ever stops flowing, things will get dicey.

That one thing? Results.

RESULTS DRIVE YOU

Results are your fuel. When they're in good supply, you're topped off for the next adventure. They guide you and keep you on track. They are your power source and validation.

Thankfully, you've seen many come your way.

Your wife responded when you made the bed, fixed the leaky gutter, or took out the garbage. She remembered how you put up with a difficult boss so you could hang onto that job. You received a pat on the back, a smooch on the cheek, or a verbal affirmation.

Your husband noticed how hard you work. He even thanked you for bringing home some of the bacon. He observed how you invest in the children. He pointed out how much he liked the new haircut (he noticed!). These are simple things, but important payoffs for the effort you've put in.

Sales rocketed after you implemented the new strategy. You poured your heart into that sermon series, and folks lined up afterward to share how it ministered to them. You worked late, and your boss surprised you with a bonus. Your kids actually thanked you for the dinner you bought them, the sports league you funded, or the vacation you planned. Your students engaged in the discussion. Your mom paid you a genuine compliment. Your dad told you he was proud of you.

You took action and saw results. This tempts us to adopt a microwave mentality. We see a correlation between effort and reward. It's like magic. Energy goes in, results come out. It's glorious.

Our baseball metaphor serves us well here. You took a swing, connected, and the ball sped into the outfield. Right in the gap. Stand up double. The fans cheered.

RESULTS CAN HIDE AND DECEIVE

But it doesn't always work this way, does it? Sometimes, the same swing is a whiff and you strike out. There are areas in your life—major, meaningful areas—where the effort-to-result ratio is completely out of whack.

You're hustling, working, experimenting, and pushing. Despite all the effort, the new business venture remains in the red, and creditors are calling.

You have poured years of effort into your marriage, but still it's unfulfilling and loaded with tension. You don't see a light at the end of this tunnel.

You've reached out to that wayward child through every possible means of communication. Yet, the text thread is still one-sided. An empty plate sits at your holiday dinner.

You're the mom of young children. You keep trying to convince them to obey, but you find yourself repeatedly pulling the same tricks out of your hat, to no avail. You're the dad who wants to communicate with his teenagers but you are bewildered as every conversation ends in a fight.

You're trying. There's no lack of effort. Just a lack of results. It seems like your life's ledger has only debits, no credits.

You're on the precipice of giving up. You know patience is part of the fruit of the Spirit. You have read how God blesses the faithful. But patience is in short supply. Faithfulness seems like a hamster wheel leading you nowhere.

FAMOUSLY IMPATIENT

Abraham is one of the most famous characters in the Old Testament and in the history of the nation of Israel. He's a dominant figure in the book of Genesis, mentioned dozens of times from Genesis 11 through Genesis 25.

He's well regarded for doing many great things. But, like most of the Bible characters we know (and like us as well!), he also made some unfortunate choices. Arguably the biggest: not waiting on God.

You may recall the story. He and his wife were told by God that they'd have a son. That wasn't all. God included amazing and wonderful promises, such as land and descendants as numerous as the stars. Then, to top it all, God told them the whole earth would be blessed through Abraham. Most Bible readers and scholars agree, this was a reference to the future Messiah, Jesus Christ.

Despite the miraculous visitations and dreams, time when by; and Abraham and his wife, Sarah, grew impatient. They knew the promises. They'd heard from God. They'd talked with angels. Still, they wanted to move things along, so they chased a shortcut.

In the end, the plan they hatched—Abraham would father a child by his wife's slave—went explosively awry (Genesis 16). Once God fulfilled His promise, Abraham and Sarah had two sons, and the descendants of those boys have been fighting each other for thousands of years. Their impatience has left a conflict-riddled mark on humanity to this day.

PERSEVERING DESPITE OUTCOMES

Galatians 6:9 contains a bold challenge and a beautiful promise. It reads, "Let us not grow weary in doing good, for in due season we will reap, if we do not give up." (Galatians 6:9)

You read a verse like that and shrug your shoulders. Maybe that works for some people. Not me. You have said, more than once, "If I'm not going to make progress, what's the use?"

That's a pivotal question. Embedded within it are two keys to developing patience.

First, you think you know what progress looks like. Sales growth. Obedient children. United family. Good health. You and I have defined what "success" means. Therefore, we "know" if we're getting closer to it or drifting farther away. That's not all bad, but it can be misleading.

We only keep going when the results are there—and we like them. We'll be a loving husband as long as the dinners are tasty, finances are comfy, and the bedroom is spicy. You will be a kindhearted wife so long as your husband keeps working hard and tackling the honey-do lists (with no attitude). We want results, and our enemy convinces us to only put our best foot forward when those results are rolling in.

Second, you believe that nothing's happening until you get *those specific results*. How can my marriage be getting stronger during times of struggle? How will my family be unified if no one is here for Thanksgiving? How will we know our new strategies are working if donations are down or sales are sluggish?

Yet, it's in these very dilemmas when patience is perfected.

A business leader and close friend of mine once joked, "Man, only a dumb person prays for more patience! As soon as you pray for that, everything comes to a screeching halt!"

We chuckled as we both acknowledged that's how patience works. The fastest route to patience—wait—did you read that last phrase? The fastest route. Am I the only person who's ridiculous enough to want *the fastest route* to patience? Is it just me? Can I get a witness?!

Moving on.

The fastest route to patience requires having our lives *not* move at the pace we wish. The very presence of slow-or-no-motion results is what brings forth the spiritual fruit of patience.

Said another way, a slower pace puts patience in place.

THE POWER OF INTERNAL RESULTS

Rain pours sustenance onto a garden. Light doesn't cut through light; it pierces the darkness. Muscle is built through resistance. Immunity is enhanced through exposure to the right amount of the disease.

Often, what we seek can only be found in the presence of its polar opposite.

We must lose our lives to gain them (Matthew 10:39). We must hate evil to fully love God (Psalm 97:10, Proverbs 8:13, Romans 12:9). There are dozens of other biblical examples of this paradox.

Even Hollywood regularly trots out these truths. Sean Connery, the famous actor, once played King Arthur. In the film, Arthur has an electric discussion with his archenemy, Malagant. Malagant intends to conquer a defenseless territory that Arthur had sworn to protect. He claims to be seeking peace, but on highly unfavorable terms. Malagant threateningly jabs, "Your words are talking you out of peace and into war!"

Arthur wisely replies, "There is a peace you only find after war. If that battle must come, I will fight it!" Sometimes, what we want is sitting directly behind what we do not want. We want peace, but we may need to battle for it. It often works that way.

Self-control often grows in the presence of events that make us feel like we're out of control. Generosity springs to life in the midst of deep need. Historic deliverance met Israel as they were caught between some rocks and a wet place (Exodus 14). We can only be caught when we fall. We must get knocked down to experience the joy of getting back up. Salvation found us while we were yet sinners (Romans 5:8).

When we are tempted to become impatient, it's usually right when patience is growing inside us. It's not that *nothing* is happening. Something massive is happening. We just might not be able to see it right now because it's not what we were looking for.

WHAT'S GOD DOING TO THE MECHANIC?

I have a friend named Gregg. That's not a typo. His name is cool like that.

Gregg is brilliant. He's a husband, dad, former business executive, and ministry leader. Not only has he run and grown large things, but he's also steeped in God's Word. He's a double threat: highly experienced and deeply wise. Early in my ministry journey, he shared a powerful principle with me. When our organization was still fairly new, we were talking about the work I do with fathers. He wanted to make sure I had the right perspective on problems and patience.

During a chat over coffee, he said, "Kent, you're going to have your hands in the ministry machine. You're like a mechanic. You'll get your knuckles bloodied, turning the wrench and making adjustments. Tweaking this and that. All that is good, keep doing that."

He paused a bit to let the first part sink in. He continued, "But, don't lose sight of something." Then, he pointed toward my chest. He said, "Remember that God cares more about what's happening inside the mechanic than what's happening to the machine."

He shared about how he stopped viewing difficulties (only) as problems to solve. They weren't just people to terminate, contracts to negotiate, or strategies to implement. The problems that came his way were *opportunities to become different.*

He described how we tend to see things in straight lines, but God walks us along these zigzagging, bending, twisting pathways. Along the way, not only do we solve problems, but we also pick up skills and gain confidence. We change. We get shaped, chiseled, and perfected. So long as I kept my eye on that, I would gain patience, wisdom, and joy in the inevitable difficulties of life.

Gregg has told me more than once, "Keep asking God: 'What are you trying to do *in me* through this? How do you want me to grow and be different in light of this challenge?'"

When I ask those questions, I clearly see something is happening! It may not be reflected in my bank account, relationships or donor base right now, but growth is occurring. And, it's happening inside of me.

We may be tempted to bench ourselves because the results just aren't there. But we may be looking in the wrong place. It could be that the results we've become accustomed to are only part of the story. Maybe it's those results we can't see that are the most important ones of all.

How We Get Back in the Game

Chapter Five

Call It Out

Now that you've wrestled with how or why you've benched yourself, let's shift our attention.

These next four chapters will help you stay in the game if you're tempted to exit. Or, if you've already stepped off the field, they will help you get back in.

Perhaps, one of those four temptations called your name. Fear, shame, criticism or impatience. Or, maybe it's something else. In any event, you're fighting the urge to withdraw. You don't want to bench yourself.

The first and easiest way to overcome that urge is to call out the reason you're tempted. With clarity and brutal honesty. It may seem too simple, but stick with me. This step is often harder than it looks.

CLARITY CAN BE HEALTHY

What we often do with our sin or weakness is find another name for it. We "euphemize" it. We take what is dark, ugly and ungodly, and we paint with a shade of more culturally acceptable language. When we do that, we actually sow the seeds that will keep us from overcoming it.

If I put you in front of Mount Everest and say, "Hey, how would you like to overcome something big?" You might stare at me with an awkward look. You're wondering, do I mean "climb *this very* mountain," or do I mean, "rid my life of anger" or "remove my tendency to gossip"? My vague language isn't helpful.

If we're going to *actually climb* the tallest mountain in the world, there are a myriad of things we need. A sherpa for one. Ice clamps. The right coats. A few months to spare. Water. Oxygen. A high tolerance for risk. And likely a dozen other things I don't know anything about. I'm not planning on tackling Everest soon. Or ever.

Knowing what we're trying to tackle enables us to gear up. If we're fuzzy, undefined, or clouded in our definition of the problem, we'll be similarly unclear about how to conquer it.

Ambiguity in naming the problem is one of the first enemies we must fight if we're to stay in the game.

Uncertainty leads to inaction. Confusion causes hesitation. Mystery shrouds the solution.

Here's my thesis. In an attempt to shore up our self-esteem, blame others for our problems and hide from the deep work we should be doing, we rename our issues. We come up with more sanitized and sweetened ways to identify our problems so they don't sound so bad.

Let's explore a handful of examples.

And, as you read through these, please know that they aren't offered in a spirit of judgment or recrimination. I believe an accurate diagnosis must precede the prescription for the cure. If a doctor knew you had cancer, but just called it "a boo boo" and gave you a band-aid, you'd sue him for malpractice.

Renaming our problems to take the sting away is spiritual malpractice.

And, while the cures for cancer often hurt, they're the gateway to health.

Let's diagnose a few, in the cold, clear light of accuracy. Some of these might be more regularly spotted in men or women, dads or moms, within the church or in a more secular context. I'll trust you to relate to the ones that make sense and leave the rest.

I'll list some of the problems we often encounter, but are tempted to rename. Then, I'll propose a more clear—admittedly more blunt, more painful—assessment that I think is helpful if we're going to get serious about addressing the issue.

Clearly, these aren't gospel truths. There's a lot of wiggle room here. However, I'd encourage us to observe the pattern we have to sanitize or explain what may be going on under the surface. As you read these, consider this: Could they be true? Is it possible that we're using one term to mask another?

WHAT WE REALLY MEAN?

"I want all the facts before I move forward." Could that mean, "I am afraid"?

"I'd like my marriage to be more balanced." Could you really be saying, "My spouse isn't doing his or her part"?

"I am not good with names." Is that cover for, "I don't care enough about you to even try and remember yours"?

I know men who say, "I occasionally go places online I should not." Most of them really mean, "I can't control my appetite for pornography." And, frankly, they might want to say something like, "I was unfaithful to my spouse, again." As Jesus said, even looking upon a woman with lust in your heart is adultery (Matthew 5:28).

I have heard women say, "Now, I don't mean to gossip." Yet, the prayer request they're about to share is precisely that.

Maybe we say, "I don't really have opportunities to make friends." But we really mean, "Could you all please just leave me alone?" Or, "I'm simply unwilling to take a risk and be vulnerable."

Some say, "Well, my (__insert personality profile du jour__) means that I tend to (__insert character flaw here__)." They took the test and received validation for their issues. But, they're actually saying, "I am unwilling to address my irritating behavior patterns so I'll hide behind this handy label."

I had a boss who told me, "Kent, you're a very passionate person. I love that! Only, when passion is fully dialed up, it looks just like anger." That was a kind way to point out one of my major character flaws. He was delicately communicating, "Don't let your anger with your colleagues hide behind a more benevolent label of 'passion.' In meetings, you come across mean and demanding. That's not going to serve you or the team well."

Have you ever met that "type A" person who really was "type J" (= Jerk)?! That's been me more often than I'd care to admit.

I may have stirred something in you with this list. And I'd like to reiterate—I'm not suggesting that behind every issue there is a huge lie or character flaw we're masking. There are legitimate challenges that arise which require a balanced and nuanced view of a situation.

Yet, I regularly find myself across a table from someone—or looking at that person in the mirror!—as I desperately try to help them more accurately define *the real issue*. I try to use blunt, descriptive, poignant language. I want to be clear, honest. Clarity is kindness.

I know of a man who's going through a messy divorce. What led to it was some deeply sinful behavior that he's only partly acknowledged. He would say he "made a mistake;" but in reality, he may have broken the law. And he undoubtedly abused one of his children and shattered the trust of several family members. I don't know that he'll find healing or a godly path forward without becoming ruthlessly honest.

Sugarcoating the issue only delays the healing and adds to the problem. While this can seem like a Debbie Downer way to stay in the game, it's essential!

Only when we really know our issue can we get after addressing it.

MY WIFE HELPED ME DIAGNOSE

While I was writing this book, a perfect illustration came up in our family. During a quiet moment after we put the boys to bed, my wife broached a difficult subject. She is extremely wise, and she's tactful and savvy in handling me. She said, "Honey, I have something to share that you're not going to want to hear."

Side note: Wives, notice my lovely bride's brilliance! So good.

First, we were one-on-one. She didn't bring this up at the dinner table or during the family barbeque.

Second, with that setup, she knows I'll mentally move into receive mode. "I'm braced for impact. Lay it on me."

Finally, she was sympathetic, not accusatory. Even though she was about to reveal a character flaw, she didn't deliver it as some "Ha Ha! Gotcha!" She was genuinely sad for me, even though I was the one on trial.

She shared something one of my young sons had brought to her attention. Earlier that day, he'd opened the rear door of my car and out fell one of the iPads we use for our ministry. This just so happened to occur at the same moment I was barking at my other son for his lack of speed getting ready to leave for a baseball game. I was already angry, spouting orders, hurrying everyone along and that's when my other son experienced the iPad incident.

He quickly checked to see if the iPad still worked, shoved it back in the car, and hopped in his seat. I didn't even know it happened. I was too busy yelling at my other son to notice.

Later that evening, he told my wife about what occurred. And, he asked her to tell me. He didn't feel comfortable telling me himself. He figured I'd get mad about that too, probably cut him off, rush him through his story (as I often do) and make it worse. Sadly, he was probably right.

As I reflect on this, I realize that sometimes I can be so . . .

Wait. What are you expecting to read right now?

"Sometimes, I can be so . . . passionate about on-time departure and respect for the team that I let my punctuality and overzealousness get the best of me and expect a little too much from my kids?"

What kind of garbage is that?

Let's try that again.

"Sometimes, I can be so . . . angry, selfish, and rude as a father. I can become so focused on the insignificant details of life, time, and schedule that I ramrod my agenda through without concern for those around me. When I do this, I sin against God and my family, and I'm a terrible steward of these precious lives He's entrusted to me. I set a poor example of what God is like. I cause emotional damage, and I drive those I love—children, even!—to feel like they don't matter and cannot approach me. I cut people off. I don't listen well. I have far too little self-control. I am a sinner. Sometimes, my sin spills out onto those I love the most."

There now. Isn't that "better"?

I could go on. There's more in my heart, but you get the idea. When calling out my sin, clarity needs to trump comfort.

Frankly, as I typed that, I cried. What a loser I can sometimes be.

Yet, when I'm as honest and raw as I can be about my own failure, I immediately feel the warmth of God's embrace. Hiding behind euphemisms, blaming other people, or pretending our actions didn't hurt anyone, doesn't move us any closer to reconciliation or repair.

THE LANGUAGE OF LIBERATION

This isn't fear, guilt, and shame language. It's the language of liberation!

I immediately pulled my son aside the next morning and apologized to him. I asked for his forgiveness. And, I didn't give any qualifiers. I didn't overreact because they didn't manage our departure well. I overreacted because I *chose* to overreact.

"I was impatient, rude, and pushy. Would you please forgive me?"

God promises to meet us in this humility. As James reiterated, "But he gives more grace. that is why Scripture says: 'God opposes the proud but shows grace to the humble.'" (James 4:6, NIV)

Paul reveals a blunt self-assessment in Romans chapter 7. He says, "For I do not understand my own actions. For I do not do what I want, but I do the very thing I hate." (Romans 7:15) And he caps it off with, "Wretched man that I am! Who will deliver me from this body of death?" (Romans 7:24).

As we mature, we can become the first to point out when we misplayed the situation. I was rude. I had a sharp tone. I came in looking for a fight. I shouldn't have said that. I was late. I was wrong. I didn't have all the facts.

Calling out our sin is the critical first step to staying in the game. It may seem counterintuitive. But, great players are the first to point out their own mistakes. I'm quite sure that Hall of Fame athletes review their own game film. I'm also sure, as they mature in their sport, they become the first to point out their flaws.

Chapter Six

Make It Right

You're armed with clarity. You know the issue—or issues—that must be addressed so you can keep playing the game. You have removed all sugarcoating and been bluntly honest about the work ahead. You have named it.

Now, you can take the next step and work to fix it. You want to set things right.

Before we dive into that—let's acknowledge the elephant in the room. Some of our mistakes have no simple "fix."

SOME MISTAKES CAN'T BE EASILY FIXED

You may be thinking, "I would fix it if I could, but there is no 'fix' for what I did. The mistake I made caused too much damage and cannot be repaired." Or, you may say,

"The person I hurt is no longer here. I missed my chance. Now, there's no way to fix it."

That is occasionally true. Some mistakes cannot be simply repaired. If this is where you are, hang with me. I'd like to propose two ideas that may give you hope.

Let's consider an example where you made a mistake that cost someone big time. Maybe they lost an opportunity, a friend, or a childhood. There's no way to go back in time. It's a past event, and you can't un-ring that bell. You're like the baseball batter who came up in the ninth inning. You had runners on base and could have smashed in the game-winning run. But you struck out. That's it. You failed. Game over.

In one sense, you're right. There is no fix. You cannot go back in time.

Your child's rocky upbringing cannot be re-lived. Your prior marriage may not get put back together. The job you were fired from probably won't come your way again. The words you said cannot be unsaid.

The fix is not just you writing a check to cover the costs. Oh, how you wish you could! If only it were that easy. There's no simple way back. In those cases, we have fewer options.

We can seek to repair damage that was done with sincere apologies. We can change course, and behave differently, demonstrating the depth of our newfound commitment. We can humble ourselves and ask for forgiveness, first from God, then from those we offended. If forgiveness is extended to us, what an amazing gift. We gratefully receive it and move on. If not, we must live with the consequences.

But, just because we can't go back in time doesn't mean we are stuck forever. We may be unable to fix it, but we can move on and live a full life in spite of it. There is hope beyond our mistakes. We just need to find that hope, embrace it, and live in the new reality.

REPAIRING WHAT WE CAN

While there are some mistakes we cannot remove, we can repair so many others. I believe these are more common. They are more real-time. The events are fresher, and we have a handful of options for making them right.

Let's say you became angry with your kids and spoke harshly to them last night. Perhaps I'm speaking from personal experience.

The way to make that right could look like this. First, offer a humble apology. "Kids, dad was angry last night, and I spoke harshly. That's my sin coming out. I'm really sorry about that. Will you forgive me?" Second, you chase that with a sincere commitment to do everything you can never to do that again. You didn't remove the error, but you made it right.

Maybe you cut someone off in a business meeting. The fix might involve a personal, one-to-one apology, followed by an uncomfortable first few minutes at the next staff meeting.

"Good morning everyone. Before we dive in, one quick thing. The last time we met, I interrupted Dave while he shared his perspective. I shut him down. That was not okay. I met with him and apologized. I want you all to know I'm sorry for that. That's not how I want our team to operate. You deserve a better example. Next time I do that, you're invited to throw something at me. All right, what's first up on our agenda today?"

You were late coming home from work—for the 100th time—and the fix *is not* just one more sad, throwaway, "Sorry I'm late; work is so busy" comment. Instead, you pull your assistant or a colleague in on the play and tell them, "Hey, I've told my wife I'll be home in time for dinner. If you ever see me working at 5:30 again, will you tell me to get outta here?"

MAKING IT RIGHT FOR CHRISTMAS

There was a time in our family when a mistake was followed by a grand move to make things right. We can laugh about this now, but not when it happened. It was anything but funny at the time.

April and I were offered a once-in-a-lifetime trip to Israel with the bill covered by a missions organization. Because of that, our four children had to stay back home for ten days. To make the trip work, we needed a ton of help from a whole cast of characters. Grandparents, aunts, uncles, and friends all chipped in.

They fed our children, kept them safe, and ran them to school and church. My wife was kid-logistics-queen, coordinating a robust schedule to make all this happen. While we were in Israel, we kept our eyes open for gifts we could bring back to thank these amazing people.

One day, we met a Jerusalem shop owner named Zak. We'd hit the jackpot. Zak sold the most exquisite, hand-carved nativities made from local olive tree wood. He didn't have enough of the kind we needed in the shop, so he grabbed his keys and beckoned us to follow him.

We wound through the narrow streets until we arrived at a nondescript door at the base of a small building. He unlocked it. April and I looked like Nicholas Cage at the end of *National Treasure*. The room was filled with an array of hand-carved statues, glassware, clothing, and jewelry. The mother lode.

April is an amazing gift giver. She sorted through her options until she had mentally matched eight nativities each with a specific recipient back home.

Getting them back intact was no small feat. Zak gave us a huge stash of bubble wrap. I packed them carefully in a large suitcase. I fully expected to find a few broken when we arrived home. But, to my delight, they arrived in perfect shape!

We examined them, but re-wrapped them and stored them downstairs. It was late October. These would make wonderful Christmas gifts. Olive wood from Israel? What could be better?

April placed all eight of them inside a large white bag in our basement near where she wraps Christmas gifts. They were in a wicker basket. Not too far from the other wicker basket that we use as a trash bin. Notice that last part.

Yes. It happened.

A few weeks later, April bounded downstairs gleefully to unpack them and begin wrapping each one for Christmas. Not seeing the white bag, she asked our teenage son if he knew where it was. One of his chores was to take out the garbage each week.

"Jonathan, have you seen that big white bag we brought back from Israel? It had some gifts in it."

Jonathan asked, "Was it sitting by the garbage basket in the basement?"

A cold, dark wind blew through the Evans house. I think I heard a black crow call out.

"Yeah! That's the one." She was not at all expecting what he would say next.

"Um. I threw that away. With the garbage. A couple weeks ago. I thought . . . it . . . was full of trash."

I can only recall one time in all our years of marriage when my wife jumped in a car and drove off. I had no idea where she was going or when—if!—she would come home.

Upon hearing these "priceless" Christmas gifts had been thrown in the trash, she bolted out the door, a mixture of sadness and anger welling up. These weren't just *any* gifts! They were from the streets of Jerusalem. We'd hand-picked them for specific people. We'd journeyed on the adventure to Zak's secret stash. They were hand-carved! Olive tree wood!

As she peeled out, Jonathan and I stood in silence. We were stunned.

He was confused, thinking, "Why would mom sit a large white 'trash-looking' bag so close to the garbage container?" April returned a while later, and gave Jonathan a piece of her mind. She pointed out that he probably was moving too fast. He wasn't paying close attention. He had been careless and not operated with high enough regard for what he was doing. He had been careless.

She had a point, but my son was surprised to hear it. He didn't believe he'd been careless at all. In fact, he'd done a little bit of extra work. He took out not one, but two, trash bags that week.

I was playing referee and hostage negotiator. I was trying to keep sharp objects out of April's hands and making sure Jonathan didn't say anything to make it worse.

The next day, things began to level off. My wife and son were working through their different perspectives on how this happened and what caused it.

OWNING HONEST MISTAKES

I took the opportunity to help Jonathan see that sometimes, even with the best of intentions, we make errors that cause damage, hurt, or frustration. We may have had good motives, but delivered a bad outcome. A mark of a mature man is whether he can own those outcomes and not hide behind his intentions.

Privately, he asked me a profound and mature question. "Okay, Dad. I know I didn't purposely ditch those gifts. I don't even think I was being reckless. But, I also realize I was the one who threw them in the garbage. How can I make this right?"

We sprang into action. I just so happened to have Zak's business card. He seemed kind, and I wondered if he could help us. I texted him and explained our situation. By now, it was late November. Only a few shopping weeks 'til Christmas.

To my surprise, Zak replied immediately. The next few days were a blur of traded texts and photos as Zak snagged some new nativities and an estimate for speedy international shipping. I went to Jonathan with the news.

I said, "Good news. Zak's got near-identical replacements ready. He'll even cut us a deal on the price."

"The bad news?" Jonathan wondered.

"Well, shipping alone will be an additional $100. Grand total, making this right will cost you about $265."

Jonathan didn't hesitate. "I'm in. Tell Zak to get them here."

Now, what do you say about a 14-year-old boy who takes that approach to something that he didn't even believe he caused? That kid. What a move. I was so proud of him. That was no small amount of money, given his financial situation.

He not only redeemed a situation, but he learned a valuable life lesson. Sometimes, there's a difference between who's *to blame* and who's *responsible*. Mature, godly people accept responsibility, even if they don't feel like they are to blame. When possible, they find a way to make things right.

Do you have "mistakes" you need to own? Maybe you were selfish, angry, impatient, lustful, greedy, or prideful. You did real harm. Damaged a relationship. Cost someone time or money. Eroded the trust of a boss, a friend, or a spouse.

How can you make things right?

Chapter Seven

Leave It Behind

So far, we've explored two ways to get back in the game. First, you've learned the value of calling out the failure or mistake. Clarity fuels diagnosis, and accurate diagnosis helps us discover the remedy. Second, you have wrestled with how to make it right. Clearly, some things are harder to fix than others. But, to the extent possible, you've tried to make a situation right.

Now, let's consider a third way to get back in the game: Leave it behind. You've got to move on. As with many things in life, the concept is easy to grasp, but the execution can be hard.

In baseball, hitting a home run is simple from a physics standpoint. You just need the correct mix of bat speed, angle of impact and exit velocity, and voila, you have a home run. We can describe "how to hit a home run" on the back of a napkin. Easy to understand, but extremely difficult to pull off.

And, that is a good place to start. Why is it so hard to leave mistakes in the past? Let's explore two broad reasons. First, there is a reminder. Second, there will be other reminders.

WE HAVE AN ACTUAL ENEMY

Reminder number one: an actual enemy. He is the devil, and he specializes in reminding us of what we've done and how pathetic we were. He has thousands of years of practice at planting ideas and concepts in our heads. He is *the* reminder.

He's good at his job. He keeps an insanely accurate running list of our misdeeds, missteps, and mistakes. He can serve them up in an instant, with our sin piled high on a platter, overflowing and dripping with the ugliness of our past behavior.

He is called the accuser of the brethren (Revelation 12:10), a thief (John 10:10), our adversary and a roaring lion (1 Peter 5:8), a murderer (John 8:44), and a deceiver (2 Corinthians 11:3; Revelation 12:9). Among his tricks, reminding us of past mistakes is one he's honed and perfected over the millennia. When this happens, I can either fight or let Jesus do the fighting for me. Allow me to explain what I mean.

Sometimes, I try to fight Satan by saying, "Oh, it wasn't that bad." Or, "Well, others have done far worse." Or, "Sure, but then I did several good things which you seem to be conveniently forgetting."

I find most of that kind of fighting useless and counterproductive. I'm actually playing into his hand. As you've probably heard someone say, "Never get in a mud fight with a pig. You'll both get dirty, and the pig will enjoy it."

Instead, I remind Satan of a few things, which clearly he already knows. He just wants to see if I remember them.

I remind him that while I did make that mistake, I am redeemed (Ephesians 1:7, Galatians 3:13). I am loved (John 3:16, Romans 5:8). I am more than a conqueror in Christ Jesus (Romans 8:37). God's mercies are new every morning (Lamentations 3:22-23). Jesus already paid the price for that sin (1 John 2:2, 1 Peter 3:18, 2 Corinthians 5:21).

When Jesus was tempted by Satan in the desert, His primary weapon was God's Word. Jesus quoted truth, as Satan spouted out the lies. If I know God's Word, I can use the same tactic when Satan comes at me. When assaulted by lies, I tell the truth.

So, rather than argue with him about the nuances or details, I overcome his accusations with the truth of my eternal position in Christ. While I live bound by space and time, Satan's reality is different. He knows that time is an invention. He also knows a day is coming when time will cease to operate like it does today, and that's when his jig is up. He has tasted eternity, and he knows what awaits him.

His time is short, and he tries to leverage the past, present and future—on earth—against me. I must learn to leverage eternity against him. God isn't stuck in the process of forgiving my sins in real time. He is not surprised at what I *have done* or what I *will do*. He saw it all, before time began. Still, He sent Jesus to remove my sin from me as far as the east is from the west (Psalm 103:12).

God already forgave all the sins I committed (in the past); and, He's already forgiven all those I will commit (in the future). He exists outside space and time. Once I grasp that, this reality is a weapon I can wield to my advantage when Satan comes-a-reminding. Satan isn't reminding me of any single thing God doesn't already know. None of my sins are news to God.

I have said in my mind, and out loud on occasion, "Satan, you're right. I agree with you. What I did was despicable and destructive. Yet, Jesus reigns forever and ever, and He said, I am free. I'll take His word, not yours. Thank you, Jesus!"

To harken back to our baseball metaphor, we need to hit the next pitch or play the next play. You'll see batters who take a big swing and miss often step out of the batter's box. They'll mentally go through a brief ritual to move on. They might grip the bat, take a slow practice swing, reattach their batting glove, or adjust their helmet.

They'll use these physical motions to reprogram their minds. "It's time to move on. Yep, I missed a good one there, but that pitch is gone. Here comes the next one, and I'm gonna connect this time." In a given game, they may need to "move on" like this ten or twenty times. One of the keys to their success is this rapid-fire capacity to put misses, errors, and mistakes behind them.

SOME REMINDERS LINGER

Reminder number two: the reminders of our sin that may linger. If reminder number one is an actual enemy, other reminders might relate to my environment, situations, relationships, or even places and spaces. Sounds, sights or smells could be memory triggers for us, taking us back to the moment we failed.

For example, I may have sinned against someone, and they've been guarded and aloof ever since. They're cautious and less trusting of me. Every time I see them, I sense it and am reminded of the damage I caused. Or maybe I was rude to a colleague at work, and every time I pass his or her office, I'm reminded of the fallout from my poor choice.

It could be writing the alimony check, driving past the house, seeing the movie, or receiving the email. It may be a place. A city, a park bench, or a road. Perhaps it's a car horn, a song on the radio, or the sound of someone's voice. All these become reminders of the angry outburst we unleashed, the money we took, the pleasure we indulged in, or the time we wasted.

These reminders can make it hard to move on. They are like balls and chains we drag around, hardly aware of how we've limped to compensate, until they come into our eyes, ears, or minds. Suddenly, the past comes lurching back into the present and we're transported right back to where we were.

The reminder—our enemy, the devil—and these reminders can be formidable foes. We want to move on, but the onslaught of accusation and memories can seem insurmountable.

Yet, consider deeply what Paul tells us in his letter to the Philippians.

> *"12 Not that I have already obtained this or am already perfect, but I press on to make it my own,*

because Christ Jesus has made me his own. 13 Brothers, I do not consider that I have made it my own. But one thing I do: forgetting what lies behind and straining forward to what lies ahead, 14 I press on toward the goal for the prize of the upward call of God in Christ Jesus. 15 Let those of us who are mature think this way, and if in anything you think otherwise, God will reveal that also to you. 16 Only let us hold true to what we have attained." (Philippians 3:12-16, ESV)

Notice Paul's progression through this portion of his letter. First, he admitted that he's not perfect. He acknowledged his own flawed nature. But yet, he exhorted us toward something that he himself was also still striving to nail down fully.

Second, he more clearly described what he had grasped. The ability to move forward, not backward. He forgot what was behind. If you dive into the Greek word used there (*epilanthanomai*), you'll see that it also can mean to neglect or no longer care for.

The picture we see is that Paul no longer "cares for" that memory! Just as a plant or animal would wither without food or water, our past can sometimes fade out of view with intentional neglect. Strong's Bible Concordance adds to the clarity of this word with this expanded meaning: "to lose out of mind; by implication, to neglect." Sometimes, I remember my failures because I keep feeding them. I must learn to purge them from my mind by benevolently neglecting them.

Third, he flexed his maturity muscles just a bit. He wrote that if we're mature, we'll agree with him. We'll do likewise. He even went so far as to say that if you don't quite see it like he does, God will correct you. I love that. I worked with an executive who'd often quip, "I judge people's intelligence by how long it takes them to agree with me." So good. Go Paul.

COUNTER LIES WITH TRUTH

In subsequent verses, Paul challenged us to follow his example and to remember where our citizenship lies. Right before he did that, notice in verse 16, he exhorted us to hold true to what we have attained. As we know, Paul was writing "to all the saints in Christ Jesus," (Phil 1:1), and as such, he reminded believers to hold true to what they've already attained. What have we attained? Well, a host of things, including eternal life (John 3:16, John 5:24), forgiveness (Ephesians 4:32, 1 John 1:9), right standing and friendship with God (John 15:15) and a clear conscience (1 Timothy 3:9, Hebrews 10:22). That's just to name a few.

Paul urged us to absolutely let go of the past and, simultaneously, aggressively hold on to the future.

You can leave your mistakes in the past. You can *benevolently neglect* them. Don't feed them! They will gradually lose their strength and power over you.

Paul also reminded us in 1 Corinthians 13 that love keeps no record of wrongs (1 Corinthians 13:5). You aren't held hostage by your past. You are loved and forgiven. Press on and move forward.

Chapter Eight

Let It Transform

We have named our mistakes with brutal honesty. We made things right where possible. We left things behind and pressed on. There's only one more step we need to take to get back in—or stay in—the game: let it transform.

We don't want to live in the past, but we do want to learn from it. This can be easy to say, but tricky to do. The brutal honesty we discussed in "Call it Out" is key. If we don't get honest about our mistakes, we'll be misguided in the lessons they can teach us.

LEARNING THE WRONG LESSONS

For example, what if I were rude to my wife? Obviously, this is purely hypothetical. I would never. But, if the impossible happened, and I was *actually rude* to my wife, she might snap back at me. Again, also purely theoretical. But, let's just say I was rude and she served it back.

I could easily ignore the first part: my being rude. I can overlook my own mistake or gloss it over with, "I was just sharing my thoughts." I conveniently pick up the story at part two, where she stepped in.

The "lesson" I might learn: I never get rewarded for being honest with my wife. So, I'll stop sharing. Or, my wife becomes really prickly whenever I mention deep and meaningful topics, so, I'll keep our conversations shallow. A wrong diagnosis can cause me to learn nothing, or worse, the wrong thing.

My ability to see my role in the mix clearly is crucial to learning the right lesson. If I overlook my impatience, I may convince myself everyone else is lazy. I'm not selfish; I just have a bunch of ungenerous colleagues. I'm not distracted by technology; my teenager just asks me questions when I'm busy.

Gaining wisdom from our mistakes must begin with an accurate assessment of the mistake in the first place. When I begin off course, I'll likely land in the wrong spot.

Once we have clarity, we can begin mining the lessons from our mistakes. This can be difficult, soul-searching work, but it's usually met with untold riches of personal progress.

BEING WILLING TO GROW

One vital ingredient to being transformed: we need to bring a willingness to grow.

In her informative book, *Mindset*, Carol Dweck describes two groups of people. Generally, people either have a "fixed mindset" or a "growth mindset." Fixed mindset people believe their abilities are fixed and cannot change. Conversely, growth mindset people believe their abilities can be grown and improved over time. Fixed mindset people resist feedback, since it strikes at the core of who they believe they are. Growth mindset people cherish feedback as an accelerant to where they want to go and who they wish to become.

While it's not a direct corollary, Proverbs would say one of these mindsets is foolish, the other is wise. The fool rejects feedback (Proverbs 15:5, 18:2, 29:1). By contrast, the wise person seeks it out, listens to it, and treasures it (Proverbs 1:5, 12:15, 17:10).

I want to be the wise man who adores feedback. I want to chase it, welcome it, and allow it to shape me.

TAMING THE TONGUE

One error I've made a thousand times—to varying degrees—is becoming angry and sinning in my anger. I have been impatient. I have yelled and criticized. I have assumed I knew the facts and acted on those assumptions before I checked for accuracy. The list goes on.

I can relate to what James said about the tongue. In James 3, he used striking metaphors to help us understand the power of our tongues. He said my tongue is like a bit in the mouth of a horse or the rudder of a ship (James 3:3-4). He compared it to a match that can set a forest ablaze (James 3:5). Rudders and matches are small items but with outsized impacts. He shared that our tongue is set on fire by hell (James 3:6). It's a "restless evil, full of deadly poison." (James 3:8). Strong words!

I've often allowed my tongue to be highly destructive. Especially when I'm angry. Yet, over the decades, I've discovered some patterns to my anger and how I use my tongue in those moments. If I want to try and tame this monster, I'm wise to heed the lessons those patterns teach me.

An athlete who wants to improve will watch game films to learn lessons or discover patterns. A baseball player might observe how pitchers tend to pitch to him, or a softball player might discern what she did wrong when she made a throwing error. They're looking closely for what they did right, what went wrong, and whether any patterns have emerged.

I have done this with anger. Often, my speed-to-anger is accelerated by certain situations and inputs. A few of these include:

- Exhaustion: I'm more likely to react in anger when I'm tired.
- Speed: When I'm in a hurry, I tend to use anger as a shortcut.
- Misunderstanding: If I believe I'm not being heard, I can become angry.
- Control: When the train is going off the rails, I feel my temperature rising.
- Disobedience: If my kids are not obeying, I'm tempted to raise my voice in anger.
- Mistreatment: If I feel offended, I might resort to anger to settle the score.

LOOKING FOR PATTERNS

I've learned valuable lessons by observing these patterns. Below, I'll share a few of those. They aren't the only ones, but I think they'll be helpful. While your sin patterns may be different from mine, perhaps this will help you do your own "game film" work.

Exhaustion: I often just need more sleep. Or, I need a break from the hamster wheel of tasks, production, and deadlines. I am more apt to take a nap or a short break these days. It keeps my energy high and resets my brain.

Speed: I still have a long way to go, but I'm more frequently employing the "delayed response." If something comes at me and I'm angry about it, I wait to reply. I may write that email today but save a draft and sleep on it. Then, I'll edit it the next day before sending. I may not return that text or call immediately. Those simple time-based delays help me simmer down, gain perspective, and measure my response.

Misunderstanding: Perhaps I'm not being clear? Or, perhaps an individual I'm iterating with just needs me to backup, go slower, or ask a better question. God is patient with me, and I need to give people space to catch up and understand without insisting they snap-to my viewpoint or game plan immediately.

Control: My way is not the only way. Often, it's not even the best way. I'm learning to ask people around me, "How would you solve this problem?" Or, in the home, I need to let my idea of bedtime flex by five minutes so my son can share that whole story about his day.

Disobedience: As a dad, I've got to address areas of obedience. However, can I address them with a calm tone and a more relaxed posture? Is my angry countenance and raised voice *actually* helping my boys learn to obey? Probably not.

Mistreatment: Some people are mean to me. Some ignore or disregard me. Funny, that sounds almost identical to how we treated Jesus. He died on the cross. But, I might have to be overlooked for a speaking role or have friends who don't text me on my birthday. The (usually petty) offenses against me need to be put in perspective. I can learn to overlook an offense, as Proverbs teaches (Proverbs 19:11).

Again, your mistakes, and thus the lessons you learn from them, may be far different from mine. But, we're in the same boat in one sense: we're both fools if we don't let our mistakes inform and transform us. As Henry Ford said, "The only real mistake is the one from which we learn nothing."

A TALE OF TWO INTERACTIONS

An interaction with a leader at a company where I worked taught me a valuable lesson. He and I had meetings that went very differently in the span of just two working days. On a Friday, we were in a planning session that involved some significant differences of opinion. There were a handful of us, and we were exchanging divergent viewpoints. It was thoughtful, challenging, and honest—but productive. We landed in a good place.

Then, in an abrupt shift, on Monday, he and I were on a different topic. However, that conversation descended into yelling, name-calling, and, on his part, the use of some choice words for emphasis. He and I were generally collegial and quite collaborative. Monday's outcome was unsettling and confusing.

I slept on it for a couple days. Then, I asked if I could stop in and chat. After a few minutes of pleasantries we both acknowledged our less than pleasant interchange, and we each apologized for our roles in the escalation. In a moment of inspiration (I should do this more often!), I posed a question that unlocked a game changing lesson for me.

I asked, "In our Friday meeting, we had a vibrant debate. It was fruitful. Even though we clearly had a difference of opinion. But, on Monday, not so much. That was a train wreck. What did I do on Monday that caused us to end up there? How was my approach different from the one I used before? Coach me." I genuinely wanted to know how or whether I led us to such a turbulent place.

He said, "You know, Kent, we pay you to push and prod. That's part of your role. So, when you debate or challenge, we welcome that! However, Friday, you were open to the possibility that someone in the room might have an idea better than yours. We didn't, so that one went your way. But, on Monday, you seemed to suggest that if we didn't agree with you, we must be idiots."

He closed with, "Sometimes, you are defensive. When you go there, you send the not-so-subtle message that if we don't see it like you do, we must be stupid. But none of us are stupid. You're short-changing your influence when you take that approach."

That stung a little, but I had asked for it. I thanked him for his openness; and a few minutes later, I left his office.

Then, I replayed memories of when I'd done that same exact thing dozens of times before. Actually, there were probably hundreds. I just couldn't remember all of them. I brought a passion to my job that could be productive and contagious. At the same time, it could veer into becoming condescending, defensive, unproductive, and arrogant. He helped me see that.

So, what about you? What lessons have you learned from your mistakes? What lessons are still buried in the ground, unharvested from mistakes have you recently made. They're there, ready for the taking, but you might need to dig a little to find them.

Perhaps, you need to ask someone who was with you when you made the mistake. Pose a similar question. Ask about your role in the issue. See if they'll be bold and candid with you about how you can avoid the same mistake in the future.

Maybe it's a boss. Your wife. A close friend. One of your older children. They probably see the lesson before you do. They know how you can let it transform you.

When you arrive at this place—where you earnestly seek feedback and input—and you let it soak into your heart and mind, you're right where you need to be. You can let the game of life transform you; and, as you do, you'll find the strength to stay in the game. When errors become your teacher, you'll have an endless supply of growth opportunities!

Call them out. Make things right. Leave baggage behind. And, let your mistakes transform you.

Never bench yourself again.

Keep going.

Epilogue

A Word to Parents

I work in the parenting arena. Specifically, with fathers. I would like to add a brief word to parents. I think the topics we're addressing in this book are uniquely appropriate to parents.

There are two reasons for this. Let's look at those reasons briefly, then unpack them a bit more.

First, we must set an example of how to stay in the game ourselves. Or, how to get back in it when we've been out for a while. This pattern-setting is more powerful than we realize. Below, I'll share why I think it's a key that unlocks many other areas of parenting effectiveness.

Second, if we've taken the first step, we are especially empowered to show our children how to do the same. Our children will make their own mistakes. They'll be tempted to give up and quit. If we've been in their shoes, we can help them lace back up.

Let's take a deeper look at how this dynamic plays out.

First, when you hear "set an example," let me encourage you *not to hear* something. Don't hear, "Do it perfectly." If that's the example you're thinking of, I want to encourage you to disassemble it. At the risk of repeating myself, don't hear, "For me to set an example, I just need to do it right all the time so everyone can see precisely how it's done. Flawless execution is my goal when setting an example."

Tim Brown won a Heisman Trophy as a wide receiver at the University of Notre Dame. He went on to have a stellar NFL career. He credits one of his college coaches with having a huge positive impact on his career. A new coach came to Notre Dame named Lou Holtz. Mr. Holtz went on to have an amazing coaching career, which included an undefeated season and a national championship.

At one practice, Holtz became frustrated with Brown, who was having trouble properly catching punts. So, Holtz stepped in and said, "I'm going to show you. Punt the ball!" The players thought this was a bad idea, but dared not intervene. The punter lofted a ball toward Holtz.

Recalling the event during an interview, Brown said, "He's out there with his glasses on, and he's going back and forth. Finally the ball comes down and breaks two of his fingers." Brown and his teammates wanted to laugh, but they knew better. He concluded one interview by saying,

"They rush him in and he comes back with a big old cast on and says, 'C'mon, let's get back to it.' That was Lou Holtz. He tried to teach you even to the point of breaking his fingers. After the fact, it was really funny, but it wasn't funny at the time."*

Now, did Coach Holtz go out there hoping to break a finger so he could teach a lesson about courage, perseverance, or grit? No, he meant to *actually catch* the punt. His objective was to succeed. To do it right. But, in what one might call a failure, he ended up teaching an even more important set of lessons to his team.

He cared enough to try. He would show them how it's done. He would get back after it once he failed. He would keep going through the pain. He would be willing to push them to become their absolute best. He was willing to—literally—take one for the team.

For the record, Holtz said in an interview later that despite breaking his finger in four places, he did catch the ball. So, it wasn't a complete loss! But, he also said that he never tried that again. Lesson taught, and lesson learned.

As parents, we are putting on a daily demonstration of how to live. Some days, we'll get it right (or at least come

---

* https://www.wndu.com/content/sports/Tim-Brown-shares-hilarous-Lou-Holtz-story-511680792.html

close). Other days, we might break a finger trying. Physically or metaphorically. How we react to those fumbles will teach our kids even more than how we handle the clean catches.

If we could be perfect parents—what a joke!—we would never be able to show our kids how to recover from failure. If we never show our kids how to recover from failure, they'll develop a twisted view of how life works. "I guess, you just live perfectly like my mom and dad, then, life is easy."

That viewpoint will only set them up for regret, shame, guilt, and confusion. Nobody lives a perfect life, and we do well to wisely let our kids into this discovery as they age. Share with them, again with wisdom and in age-appropriate ways, how you have fumbled. Times in your past when you got it wrong, blew the opportunity, or sinned against someone. Seasons when your priorities were out of whack. Battles the devil brought your way. Wrestling matches you've had with God.

Ditch the concept of "perfect parenting." It only hobbles our children and gives them a warped view of what to do when they inevitably run aground on the rocks of life.

This leads us to being in a position to coach our kids when they go through life's hard knocks. If we've been knocked off the horse and climbed back in the saddle, we have a story to tell. We have deep wisdom to share. We have encouragement to bring.

In his second letter to the Corinthians, Paul says, "Blessed be the God and Father of our Lord Jesus Christ, the Father of mercies and God of all comfort, who comforts us in all our affliction, so that we may be able to comfort those who are in any affliction, with the comfort with which we ourselves are comforted by God." (2 Corinthians 1:3-4 ESV).

Consider the purpose statement in verse four: "So that we may be able to comfort those. . . ."

God brings us comfort through our trials, challenges, and mistakes, but not so we can simply rest in the comfort and enjoy it. There's that, to be sure. But we also can comfort those who are in any affliction.

We give comfort because we've been given comfort. We are conduits of comfort. Messengers of mercy who share with the afflicted that God is for them and wants to walk through the fire with them.

A key reason we need to stay in the game is to set a godly example. This doesn't mean we get every moment perfectly right. It does mean that when we do fail or when life comes at us with all its unnatural fury, pain, and temptation, we stay in the game.

Just by staying in—or getting back in—the game, we are setting an example.

And, that helps our kids learn the valuable lessons presented in this book.

Don't bench yourself. This will help your kids learn not to bench themselves either.

Keep playing.

WHAT'S WITH ALL THE BASEBALL REFERENCES?

We realize this book contains dozens of baseball references. We also recognize baseball is a bit like an "inside joke" America is playing on the rest of the world. If you're from the USA, you probably caught (one more!) these metaphors. But, if you're from elsewhere, some of the lingo may have been more confusing than helpful.

We created a resource just for you!

If you need some help baseball jargon, and if you already know a thing or two about soccer – and if you're up for a laugh – go snag our handy "Baseball – to – Soccer Cheat Sheet". It'll clear up any misunderstanding.

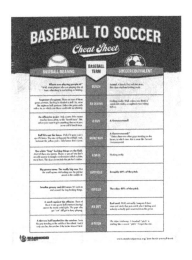

BUY *DON'T BENCH YOURSELF* FOR YOUR CHURCH, TEAM OR COMPANY.

Maybe you know of a group that would benefit from the message of this book? You're a business executive, pastor, small group teacher or coach who leads a group that could use some encouragement.

Snag multiple copies of *Don't Bench Yourself* at a large discount. You can go to the website below, or touch base with us directly.

To place a bulk order, go to
www.manhoodjourney.org/bench-bulk

Got questions or need more info? E-mail us at
info@manhoodjourney.org

MANHOOD JOURNEY HELPS DADS BECOME DISCIPLE-MAKERS
Are you a father who wants to intentionally disciple his children?

If you're a father, you know raising godly children is a difficult but rewarding challenge. Don't go it alone. And don't try it without God's power!

We can arm you with an array of resources to help:

- Group and 1on1 Bible studies
- The *Father On Purpose* podcast
- *Mountain Monday* weekly newsletter
- Free eBooks, Reading Plans and more!

Gear up at www.manhoodjourney.org

OTHER BOOKS FROM MJ PRESS

Christian books written to help men, fathers and leaders thrive

Our ministry publishing arm, MJ Press, produces books to help men grow and thrive as fathers, husbands, and leaders. If you'd like additional books on how to become a godly man, husband, or father, check out these other titles.

Bring Your Hammer: 28 Tools Dads Can Grab from the Book of Nehemiah

More Than the Score: Cultivating Virtue in Youth Athletes

Wise Guys: Unlocking Hidden Wisdom from the Men Around You

Receive: The Way of Jesus for Men

www.manhoodjourney.org/mj-press

PRIVACY.FLOWCODE.COM

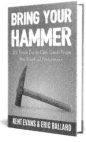

ANGER FREE DAD

A course for building a more peaceful and connected family

If you struggle with anger, you are not alone. Anger is cited as a top struggle for dads. Sadly, when we blow our top, it fractures our relationships with our kids, models ungodly behavior, and, left unchecked, can impact them for a lifetime.

However, God's Holy Spirit can lead us to peace and joy. By knowing and applying Biblical principles, we can see our actions and words become a blessing to those around us.

Our **Anger Free Dad course** helps you learn how to root out your anger and become a calmer, more patient father. Ready for a change? Your wife and kids will thank you for it.

www.manhoodjourney.org/anger-free-dad

FATHER ON PURPOSE PODCAST

A podcast for dads that is biblical, practical and fun.

We produce the Father On Purpose podcast to encourage and challenge dads to step fully into their calling as godly leaders. We strive to make it biblical, practical and fun.

We've had some amazing guests on the show: Gary Chapman, Chip Ingram, Stephen Kendrick, Ken Blanchard and Brant Hansen, to name a few.

We don't have all the answers, but we believe God does! Let's explore them together.

www.manhoodjourney.org/podcast

Made in the USA
Middletown, DE
09 September 2024